T0108621

Disbound

KUHL HOUSE POETS

Mark Levine and Emily Wilson,
series editors

Disbound

poems

Hajar Hussaini

University

of Iowa Press

Iowa City

University of Iowa Press, Iowa City 52242
Copyright © 2022 by Hajar Hussaini
uipress.uiowa.edu
Printed in the United States of America

ISBN 978-1-60938-867-6 (pbk)
ISBN 978-1-60938-868-3 (ebk)

Text design and typesetting by Omega Clay

No part of this book may be reproduced or used in any
form or by any means without permission in writing
from the publisher. All reasonable steps have been taken
to contact copyright holders of material used in this
book. The publisher would be pleased to make suitable
arrangements with any whom it has not been possible to
reach.

Printed on acid-free paper

Cataloging-in-Publication data is on file with the Library
of Congress.

To my sisters with/out whom I has no meaning

Disbound means that the book or booklet, whether printed or manuscript, was once sewn and bound, but has now lost its binding. The term may be distinguished from "unbound," which means that the book was never bound.

Oxford Reference
*A Dictionary of English Manuscript
Terminology: 1450–2000*

contents

notes from Kabul

on being fine when others aren't;
notice graphic, how quotes
wax truth & assassinate
anecdotes

the surplus of survival
guilt covers pages & the data
at the price of two
boiled eggs

rectangular streets grind us
like watercolor powder
we wash blood off bags
& hats & the few

branches of tree
are in blaze yet we
still play stone scissor
paper

losing sight

                    a screw in my glasses
came off   fell down the hill
I lost sight of a valley 5,000 years ago
I climbed to see   a city on top
          instead, everything
was in square colored pixels
                    like a low-quality picture
I have of Kabul in the '70s
                    impermanence—missing
of a boarding call in an airport
                         discovery of a lie
after a commitment is made
                    a T blows himself up
in the midst of a ceasefire
blind among the mob of angry men
                    lynching Farkhunda
          a woman wearing jeans
beneath a burqa
a man who loved you more
                    who loves you less

inventory

animals and other existences attempt
to retain an inventory

of memories stashed cool and dry
in the mind's cooking place;

accumulations are locked behind
a person who has left; the emigrant

has an authority over
the substance to be disposed;

the harshest items unlabeled;
donated to public officials

       triumph is a permit

the state of affairs chauffeurs the thousands
out of place; deviates from a modern tourist

itineraries are narrowed
down and have no such address of return;

the views lying across your eyes
are worth noticing; sky is clouded; in this hinterland

each house is concrete; roads are thickly
asphalted; no visible destruction;

perhaps the best thing about evacuation
is learning how-to optimism

       they will tell you that there is a way back

anatomy endangers the concept; your ankles
are wobbly; hands refuse the complications

shoved in your sleeves; not framed or filed;
but squeezed into screws of everyday glasses;

the processes; in friendship
we become friendly; anxious we have anxiety;

when we are placed in a fragile expanse
do not we become broken; unhealable;

shifting positions; shake an immigrant
and scraps of paper fall out of reality

on our chest planes

Dead white clothing is a better title. Laylami sounds more like a
flower. We find charming boots, jumpers, summer dresses, anti-
age cream. The Bush Bazaar carries brand names & ankle socks.
Smuggled from nato camps, the items possess finer qualities
made in Vietnam, in Sri Lanka. The documentary I
watch brings up dignity. "What does it mean for the
third world?" Third is not a place. It's a project
of us going through the fabrics. Learning the ratio of poly.
Natural, not part of the new economy, we worry only
about affordability & whether one wears
such a thing in an Islamic republic.
I think about those days. I think about traveling back.
The first task is what I need to deport: Sarah says *bring
a squirrel* / Kowsar is interested in *a violin* / Zohra needs *everything*.
I call them, phonetics in the air, facetiming a monotonous Farsi
song composed on the meaning of memory as a *faculty by which
the mind stores information* & the meaning of
distance as *an amount of space between two things or people*.
Distant & remembering.
These international calls elevate me,
Baba mountain range, frequencies of my sisters'
voices. I'm informed that a man has detonated a thing
at my cousin's clinic. My first friend attempted to cut her wrist. My
father may die before the files are processed & they need to
get going.

the property of being separate

pause   after the first vowel of this name   imagine an apostrophe   cutting it
in half   wait   for the jarring syllable of a biblical woman bearing a prophet
child as a slave a second wife   in the absence of g an entire alphabet runs
after j   a hebrew name morphs into a jerusalem anarchy   gathers stones
in a desert   incarcerates dissent through a phone call   ringtones are famed
for shifting moods   these organs should throw   a security council

refuse the gospel   the name was only picked for its uniqueness
semite eyes full brows but if shortened the *hey-ch* sound   meaning
nihilism per persian linguists   or extended the *jay*   blue feathered
bird in the rhythm of choice   was I this other   a cosmopolitan is quick
to point out that's interesting   it's the assigned alien number
one has to fill in every form   that crawls underneath skin

apostrophes are not only operators of possessing   they necessitate a casual
way of pronouncing   sometimes I just want to go by h'j but then
an uncanny ghazal cases my subconscious   do you want pistachios
and/or almonds   paying me a visit at every balcony I stand to smoke
reciting poetry with her muffled voice   calling me back to a country
I cannot afford to call home   anymore

phantasmagoria

the magic was brought into
the store by an old woman
whose migration followed
cutting down jasmine trees
in a chest with two holes at its bottom
the rug entombed a discoloration
its tassels worn and loose
hung like meat fibers over flame
on the bus back I met the Little Prince
across the aisle a weeping woman
one of the three angels
in a Shamlu poem

tea house

please oil the door   that creaking sound   wellbeing
at one or both ends   bolt shape hole   piercing
silver nor gold neither   palmistry science   at parlor's shop
where we went after   chaikhana   asking to hang
our bleeding   jackets   humid
shorr rus shorr rus baran   second by second   I counted beats
praying for bodies that remained   infinite water
               lemon tea honey please

the photography of home

ivory doves return to the shrine in Mazar-i-Sharif
a woman takes the weight off   the bird lands
on her brown burqa showcasing sunflower seeds
her open palm [   ] a thousand
blessings

the familiar brown body of a teen   pulling water
from a well   &   Salsal's embezzled eyes
shy away from his axed leg   the boy's potato
land frontier [   ] casting off
pharaohs

plump eyelids & juvenile fists   are ichor
wears henna circles & is married to [   ]
an infant   &   letting the sheer   display
her gray   trembling in snow she conceals
the grotesque

three men sipping chai siya on Kandahar Road
returnees rummage a clean bathroom   & van
drivers joined by a coriander Karzai's kingdom
[   ] five hundred kilometers the cassette
tapes rave

& Kababs jabber   now strange I pulled myself
out of the map & soaking sugar lumps [   ]
luster paper sheets fly in thick flock   I carry
broken feathers   forage for filling the void
I prescribe English

bombast: a Persian etymology

Sherry ranks tapestries of cinnabar that *became* beige.
Imagine peris caravan in a *path* of baksheesh. Pashm
shawls, taffeta cassock, a qalandar in bulbul bazaar:
samosas, pilafs, pistachios, caviar & lemon candies.

Roxanne tambourines. Margaret has prophet flowers.
Jasmine sitars. In the magic kiosk: we have naans &
divans, bronzed talc *face*, orange *lips*. Paradises
are pajamas in seersucker & *high* percales. Scarlets

are not *only* for sultans in durbar who bezoar the tiger.
Assassinate markhors, a carcass of jackal, simurgh &
musky manticore should have been mummified, *kept*
in serdabs, zirconiated & sugared. India is a lilac.

Sandalling a galingale with bedeguar. She has a scimitar
a carafe, chinas & *sleeps* in a khaki baldachin. A chess
mate is after the spinach & *calm* serendipity in douane.
Leave her barbican *alone*. Her taj is a tiara, *gemstoned*.

road trip

is an extension
        movement of the right hand
        with multiple pinched
nerves, a syndrome
        of being out the window
        waiting for a gust
            the odyssey is his
            driving us
I am only taking notes, browsing maps
        seemingly they are
                moving us
a quarter-tone scale
        curves my predisposition
        of being held
in a historical maternal scent
        to get a glimpse of her grass
        colored eyes
            if I close mine
            to the numb-
er of miles
        the secret of lending
                credence
to a ghostly appearance, carry
        a night dream
        into a discussion of what happened
and scrub it off
        only after your teeth are clean
        by the faculty of retrieving

I held her jaw in my palms
liquids barely circulating her body
in this language the body
is both
alive and not
if I were to choose
the strongest sense, touch
with its ability of measuring
its intelligence of distance
his ear to his chin is long
for five inches
outside five silent hyphens
pour over wallpapers
scarecrow fireflies the barnyard
how the same grammar
dictates
my east splits volumes
from its collective subject

funeral

I sit down   in funeral attire
as recitals beat my eardrum   a mosquito
flies over the stash   of Quranic chapters
in gendered halls a bird pecks   my nerves out
in mourning a mother   nenuphar grows
under your chin   your body is a gutter
-overflow   I wish this cemetery
was an open field   a leafless garden
my sister tells me   outside is many people
inside three daughters   unwed
the thirst for afterlife   our mother

Sufis instead

do not speak
in fragments my drunken
lunatic let's limp
patterns of assumptions
you're not eating
just caffeine & cohol
my religion al-prohibits
asking for favor, gambling
on pounds you've been losing
my brahmin let's become Sufis
instead, I'll read you Persian poetry
in translation my soul is a print
where are you going? what language
are you speaking?

on-site commands

the holy month brought
helicopters & lit ambulances

the graves despoiled of skeletons
made a profit margin

wrapping corpses fell
out of fashion by the time police

cars three four hours settle in
a cameraman & a well-known

columnist are at odds over
who gets to report this first

the field of death

tell her stories of Kabul's golden age when girls
wore miniskirts and boys sold Elvis—tell her
about Mazar's sheer pira melting in cold
chai.

she is wearing a floral scarf and orange poppies
grew in Kandahar—because the two blue stones
beneath her brows complement freckles of the
civil war.

she is sitting on a backyard bench holding
onto an easy question—faculty of sounds in this
city mourns after each explosion since God
existed once in each unit of this ministry.

incumbencies' dispatch

the nth life

again a man in a suit
wrote an article that measured grief
I thank the special force, he said
& the percentage
of glasses that didn't
break & I address
a holy constitution
like the Quran or America
whichever works an interchange
our country is un-rulable
by the beard & sweet dream
are made of this

the reformer's dead end

in absence of an engineering mind
the ambience of peace is semi
transparent & by no means
a lawless correspondence
has prestige
when five thousand
evacuate this calendar
will be ours & there is nothing
unless there is a finalized
thing I think
mutual terror has guinea pigs
Ts are limitless and As & Ts
are neither program-based
as for the bleeding
we should compromise
perhaps shut our tongues
& if required count
each hair strand

simple café

among the lost generation of Simple going   Café drinking
your former lover orders a cup of tea   whose current lover
                        a lemonade

Kabul has only one place with close distant tables & chairs

the soundtrack a spaced repetition   between the introvert
on her smartphone   & the extrovert thinking
                  about a thrown grenade

the unspeakable gerund of a suicide jacket

urban correspondents

tokhu nesti at occupied eight am this building
and its employees were a target—it's a component
that the loaded coat is next to the football stadium

—outside the green zone a damaged spirit
was found the spokesman briefed that civilians felt
the demand of going back to normal

tokhu nesti the national army is overgrowing
the security state is an indecisive cutter & stitcher
of a fabric that the Ts are a part of—

tokhu nesti the impunity enjoyed by forty countries
dances with every beat—as with all rounds of talks
the minister of defense is a convoy with blue eyes

tokhu nesti a hundred and fifty tried to escape
from the gate—the flames they say burned every
document as an act of surveillance

ask a population of independents what to do with
this criminal? tokhu nesti is an organized violence—
in becoming a savior one needs the course of actions

an account, unconditional postures—don't worry
this city plans to be

telephone calls from PD #3

strange—they struck the leafy trees
those diplomatic quarters: binamoos
chuckled at this rushing hour of commute

hey boy
come here nobody allows me

[I don't know where the shooting
                                    ]

clouds confiscate
my head & face burning
hurry up bodies
through haze
a girl appeared who said

                [it was so very loud]

you . . . heard it, right? yes. the alive
escaped—the benevolent
& benevolence dispersed

there's no other news, look:
here's our commandant

inverse of most stories

murad khane once built for the mundane ancient court
who is right, and who is wrong, left of the old city
are long dog battles and bird markets, on carpets
octagons in red

there were days men would have paid for love of
quail, in turquoise tonban outfits, they would bid
on female offspring, as *patience stone* has entailed
but their kinds are already soiled dead

in battlefield, on streets, in uniform or with a long
beard, an american surveillance balloon, godlike
watching a pierre cardin store opening, the snow
leopard fur, dead lives on the shelves

the chess made of marble, a new gen continuum
catwalks whereas ahmad shah masoud wore pakol
we new gen rub, and roll, grass, and we fuck
from behind, ours is the city of secret lovers

we buy light sim cards on promotion days
smile at european counterparts our parents
believed in

madar jan

to divorce from a stroke Tahira a fifteen-teen / wanting
to wear a white dress / not to get married to forty-three years'
control / grandfather's last name whose scripts were torn
by stepbrothers / a mobilized union leader / charismatic
but the silence fee bruises her arms / dams
resist an ocean's mood swings / later sugar making
the inside of her crystalized / the right bones well versed
unfamiliar to our family was the left tongue that switched
from the middle month to the doctors in Tehran / terminating
the thing with feather / best at our prayers / dispersed under
her feet a heaven / she died a few times year after until
the metaphysics signed the deal / a visitor tag stale in
my satchel / her ring around our refuged neck / guilt
swims in father

transhumance

follows the harvest of soiled
vegetations

since low land keeps warmer
colors

its air decreased of density
highlighting farmers' faces

milking cows tending eggs

all of this was happening
a flag party burned the Quran

it nicknamed Kabul

our uncles formed a resistance

seeks asylum in Iran an ancient court
as callous

in the way of Waziristan a backyard
decluttered

carter introducing us to mujaheddin
because we were not white

headlines weren't heartbreaking

no revolution was for all
the dogs had to come back

circling cell overtly fueled off
prisoners

for there were more women in the
universe

this is not part of
the sentence.

provincial heartache

in two thousand one
a slaughterhouse
was renovated
an art production built
its founding father
a photographer
against forgetting
the pillar of Panjshir

mirroring the ministry
at the turn of the century

the town's conversationalists
share noghl and tea
her brunette bangs
chapan lee
goatee and glasses
in gardens by the hundreds

a civil society
I grew in the belly of

a bubble blows the biggest
shisha loop
do not leave a trace
on disco balls
my green zone
flagged white city

the sublime a colony
emulsifying an avant-garde

how much of Kabul
do I embody
its chamber
of commerce
plays hopscotch
like a fucking
thirteen-year-old

no one waits for the janitor
to speak

in the event of murdered
colleagues
rush the sentiments
to the digital prophecy
of an occasional bombing

a country of calamity
is not a Hafez poem

nor does it wear
a waistcoat dropped
from the sky
to assist the americans
who won't count
the how many

trails connecting
the mountains are feasible

The farm men
have heard
of a soon-to-be
metropolis
in carnage
a village reminisces
pre-feudalist

an ambassador drinks
the lost names

the heeled avenues
the canopy king
of our nineteen twenties
translating texts
of living poets
salute the instinct
of staying alive
salute this marriage
between parallel parts

to eat the ideology
from which I've come

these parts keep falling
like things
for forty years
in fear
to heighten
a driving anger
the land

a hiroshima nagasaki project
of flattening hindukush

later if humans appear again
she will be in the
company of plants
having no mountains
no covert operation
and the irrigation
will be another
discussion

jocular geopolitics

how each corner
goes north amid brown
barricade beard or
underneath an oblong
blue colored veil
a hidden smile without
the laughter a tactic to
reclaim the human face
of those temporarily
safe

self-checkout

I am many people at once:
an institutional lab has
recycled the ingredients.

to supervise the wild:
spiral hair ties
& spermicide.

to be sheltered:
black raisins
& shredded carrots.

first, it was magistrate.
second, margarine.
a world of thirds.

how to walk
across the aisles:
starch on both sides.

chorus

I   hitchhike prostituting the intermediate
you   brought in
        gauze pad bandage turmeric pomade
you   brought in
        liberation from a coup d'état curse

          we   should not talk about   the ground narratives
          that have not nothing to do with our own personal lives
          this in our minds   this   is closer to us
                our methodical planet
          the connection cable   the unhappy wife of the bastard
          border   none of these   actually   matter

I   still whisper peace
      be upon tangerine
      primitively pomegranate
I   cannot speak of
      the neo-narrative

          we should echo   opulence manuscripts
          with two points in mind   admit
          the damned owned propriety   its taste of ruin
               and rhapsody   admit also
          the re-creation is a process in which we as artists
          are made to be in service   not shallow private

you   enjoy Danish pastries
      nadir of magnanimity
I   want to walk
      alkaloid and subdued
      outside

the blessed gambler

the Persian poet obsesses over the beloved's forehead
where lips are set free to fluctuate in a field
kissing the eyes till hairline

                    hurried organic joint / new age songs

the capacity to be-in-the-moment rubs off on me
I discontinue rehearsing my texts and subordinate
conjunctions appear less and less

   my lungs are large organs / the social can take a rest

because I want him like a critic yearns for a public
one kilogram of ground spice is over my heart
I respire but Kabul has baked my psychoanalytic

                    so, I've made him the nation's cuisine

   like symbols, chromosomes

the lane in an old email

against the dried out sole tree: a choreography
gripping bolly's chin, spilling in the lake
a promise of Kabul Dreams, replicating a Turk
artist, *Tamally Ma'ak*, walking as Charlie
Chaplin—O we were charming

      the collaboration of course
      bore consequence

I was the deliberately unsuccessful
inadequately taking risks, rumbling
in the presence of broad shoulders
pressing palms against the rug pile
then to be nervous was to gaze long
enough into an abyss, I never walked
a kilometer

but she . . .   she dived into the subject
of the matter   acquired the knowledge
of voting for the accused: my seditious
sister addressed the eyemove shielded
her chest and wore cherries as earrings
so what, what if we're—

      we wondered if a siblingship
      dies after one party weds

then marriage was a separation technique
we promised against the giveaways
terms were to be bended for a stranger
who could, in fact, *kiss*

      before owning our cellphones
      we were two mothers

syntactically, rules were changed: nanay
as in madar jan, as in maman, as in boboy,
benumbed, just involuntary movements
two younger girls beautiful
blue and black eyes, seven and five
Zohra and I watched and washed
in the photos it's very clear
how uncaring

beyond matters of identity two independent nouns found each other
she had left a capital flare missed the funerals and the foods
he examined the problem description attuned to fulfillment

      an entity had limned a thin line in the middle
      of their last names first they had met at a film festival

they talked about revelation the daily performance
her interior corrupt and decolonized
his body had been through a lot

      she paid attention to broadcasts in bed
      this readiness in euphemism excused the half truths
      she stuffed into chosen words worried about the resemblance

      he absorbed the world's music in shelves of diverging
      materials individual intonations that merely one
      without a background found an entrance

each safeguarded their mechanics of coping mismatched
yet the ordeal kept leaking out and the damage transpired
the tissues the notes for a poem a lute

some of the times nothing helped some of the times a finite
camaraderie in stories of being bullied and beaten
she just nodded on poverty he had nothing to contribute

some of the times one lets go of the other to see what happens
to each unmarried and the hyphen belongs to an element
feeding off cord one attempts and aborts

a distinctive duplication

three periods . . . three decades of remote arts
only periodic mystics . . . an endo-kingdom alters
the appearance of my uterus

cycles of internal bleeding . . . a doctor years later
diagnosed makes you . . . an infertile woman
you may need to hurry . . .

corresponding to possibilities of yet
another civil war breaking out . . . new waves
of displacement floating unto Mediterranean

I skim through the full circles in prose . . .
in poetry they are invasive intruding communities
removing individuals not needed . . .

in journalism ellipses are omission a cut tongue
strives for the unsayable . . . throughout my adolescence
I circled words with P

among the sounds that block the airflow
it coalesces with soft S or key sounding C and/or L
which makes a thing a common English word . . .

rarely found in Farsi and if so imported by tradesmen
like a tin of pringles . . . I copied myriads from text
books and recited them from a blue journal

its front and back covered in logos of the international
children's emergency fund . . . I drew my hatred
for the ugly notebook in symmetrical lines

on top of zigzagged horizons to create an equal
number of squares in each I carefully placed one word
. . . a frequent exercise prior to stretching myself

on a shared mattress a foreign language became
my precise measurement of stress . . . plosives
in them . . . theatrical movement of my lips . . .

I was told that my table of disembodied words
is not how learning a language works . . .
but one dissects a complex into its capsules . . .

there is a sudden release of air that follows an ellipsis' *P*
there . . . clouds are created . . . let's eavesdrop on the friction
of two unvoiced rubbing against each other . . .

as suspension points . . . or for a stuttering effect . . .
they are always together . . . if one is not fitting in
the poet is disabled

peopleless

on his leave of absence, we walked along the back bay.
I stepped backward to seize our sentimentalities & a bird
of prey soared around him. an emperor in entity, he is
the manifestation of my immeasurable needs.

he tyrannized my slumber & exploited my breast. in khaki
corduroy pants & a tee, the compulsion to check my email
lessened to once per day when he was there for seven
twenty-four-hour days.

we were in black & white. a museum of fine arts.
the *house of death* in graciela iturbide's. we *dance
at bougival*. gaze at *la japonaise*. our bourgeois passing
at marriott boston hotel begets another marital status

and the thought of it drowns me in his dark morning coffee.
because an old woman saw my destiny; I'm peopleless. my
lungs are mushroom clouds. imperial boots march on my
margins. my mammals are unloved. I'm a government

of shame. my mouth is dry & my words are all &
forever out of tune.

self-parody

the poetic order of my native tongue
is dense too romantic for the current
conditions of living   that I have no
choice but to migrate   to a violent
way of separating   my lines

meta-variable

the :ized is part of the celestial object   vis-à-vis the :ist
she discovers that her mind also thinks   form is a super
-ficial thing ears are innately reflexive   and so she listens
                    but isn't buying the total deficiency

homogeneously   an imperialized is as envious and is told
to remain seated   meanwhile she attends to what extent
the two worlds are fundamentally different   aka one is
                    under excessive stress

argus-eyed   ambivalent on justice   how one realigns
and whether she is out of line   reads the note in trans
-lation: *Only one. / The one that is more tired. / This*
                    is the instruction.

then counting the counterintuitive.   her tourist love
who claimed her country   is a land of contradictions
the grand Buddha who ate his shit   her father who was
                    both revolutionary and mechanical

home simultaneously warm and at war   marching on
monetarily dependent with checkpoints   deep down
she finds   *a voice infused / of neither hope / nor*
question   comparatively indicates a tenacious presence

day in and out this subject   in diction   in peace
punctuates   is aware of the case for :ialism   pm
writhes in her circadian rhythm   barbed wire whose
                    disentanglement should be a paid position

stress & strain: a contrariety

I conceived pain & advanced
a bigger frank divided itself into two
uneven lines in a semblance
of lips in the man who laughs
lying down at different lengths
feeding off each other
piling up
the shorter is a private
the longer is my republic

   —

  a sorrow that grips a neckline
  beats me down cheats & admits
  me to an emergency next to it I sit
  vulnerable driven from Latin
  wounded affixing its allocation
     cutting the ribbon
     ending on a preposition
     leaving tensed rooms
 grief is aware of
 its residence—time grants
    appropriate emotions
     I archive its semantics
     I earn its adjectives

     —

    larger than life one is born into
    catering to its every desolation
    so spend your days walking
    around a ruined garden notice
    the mini sprouts why rain is scarce
      watching the ceremony
      partaking in an agreement
      hanging behind closed doors
    grief is aware of
    its residence—are planted ghosts
     following you & will one of you
      ever make a difference
      hardly one dreams of being
    that person who saves the nation

45

common cause

hmm . . .
my reflection jacquard
strains of gold
        beneath the curled
                    eyelashes
god's intricate
strokes

I dust off a vision

a Saturday morning
            drowns in oral
    exasperates a global
    virus

even though I steered
clear of love

    in high altitudes
I acted as pragmatic
    subverting an animal
                instinct

disorienting orientalism

it takes to know
a departure surpasses
                    culture
        O i'm loved

blowback

indoor my proteinated pancake
dematerialized & the earth bloats
the kurds, syrian, kashmir
the refined petroleum, the strip
left is meta-forensic

a progressive prophet briefs
my mornings past the learning
curve of an ordinary reader
an area for what must be said
is already said

here: sugar-free brownies
recommended recipes from
a location where chess was
the first world game marble
of rome roadhouse for

silk I'll declare my own
thesis & see him clean
shaved standing by my
luggage we belong together
like cairo to pyramids

seizing the circumference
of my waist asks did you
bring candles to the dynasty
of nine elevenistan?
I brought the self

precedes essence

its impulses disperse throughout the social dynamic
subsequently the expressive parts of my unit shake
\ it's imperative to choose not to speak \
        anxious \ as an indication \ I could not
enunciate \x is silent\ a Russian ESL chalked in pseudo
north American accent \lectures later\ the disintegration
of novel words into no further division
            one figures meaning through
breakage and adjacent to

outside the map occupying the periphery your beliefs
are minor chords I've heard about annihilation of the self
\ it's imperative to choose that notion \
        let me describe \ what I perceive \ to be
its actions \ it saturates my incissioned foot then pulls
itself up stares into my eyeballs and then issues
so, you think you are one of them \ I wanted to get rid
             of it but it drops by the delicate
hours of my day—

maintaining a typographical distance poking me with
a pen donates me moleskin in these human conditions
\ it's imperative to read why I feel like this \
        at the bar's entrance a friend
tells me *why you won't apply for a state id you don't have
to carry this history* in his reference to the past events \
when the exteriors presented the outright complication \
         I'm told everything depends
on—

how everything should end

> *one night we will prepare a lavish meal*
> *we'll close the doors, cracks, and crevices*
> *one of us will open a gas valve*
> *by morning our passage will end*

was the film dialogue my brother delivered
filling a nylon backpack—the boat
was compact
                —we were out of power
the battery blinked
       our eyes every minute
scanned the lamps
       as though God was above

the divine camouflaged in a safe house
as soldiers did when insurgents attacked
my brother worked in the camp
             —he knew about war
won't end
       waited for his general
to write back
       years passing—case stale

I ask in Frankfurt are you dating
someone? he responds are you happy
we didn't die?

the question

uploading my responses to the question   I'll perform the privatized human well
breathing deeply with smoke-free lungs   or   continue taking my antidepressants
I've walked past death   &   stood by the entrance to deposit them my bribes
there is nothing in death worth giving   &   nothing in life worth dying for

committing to the initial question is a suicide committed to you   I'm only a fool
on the query of the free will   I fooled death for twenty years looking for the right
time like my brother said there is a right time for everything   kept in the mind . . .
second only to water in its strength   that real goalkeeper lives in the watch &

outside of it   by the time that news joined general knowledge   I found multiple
magnetic stickers on my forehead invisibly hanging   & several patches that were
steamed to my skin cloth tagging myself along advocating breath & influencing
why I should be here   air in & air out   air in & air out   air in & air out

I find the range of my sensibilities   but then an article claims a debt I must pay
to that tragic anticolonial country a mile above sea-less & landlocking the poems
in which hope persists   & cannot leave the stage of politics   & polyamorous
my partner   vastly different   yet strikingly   similar to   how I

moved across the world he sits rightly in the future frontier I hope no one arrives
in his heart again

proctoring

in a previously vacant hall, students concentrate on passing a theory test, and as time, in a traditional clock, analogs, one person complains, accounting is the art of keeping, silent, upper classes are aware of this, the algorithm is simple, I stare, at young faces, white walls, each one promising and blank, among them one fabricates a mustache out of chemically dyed hair, someone chews on a drawstring, I see one person squeezing an inflamed cyst, there has to be a taker who doesn't give a shit,

whose relaxed position occupies, a culture of cool, maybe this work is a path of worshipping, in hadiths, I remember, Allah, the god in question, loves beauty, boredom is beautiful, and a minaret is a cohort of both, I sat there, unfaithful, outside the testing center, to gaze is to say everything in my east is east, to have is to suggest a heartland theory, to havenot is a failed state, a coup toward an aimless independence,

in this morning geography, I think of a sandstone statue who belonged to a central province, the lords filled his belly with bomb and the kids with rubbish, the dynamite that caused an outcry was the exam, in which, i came of age, and, a giant balloon soon appeared over my head, as for pay $15 an hr, fair is a child fascinated by the science of fears, guerrillas, and, not ever buying another pair of jeans,

the quotidian

'an Iranian museum holds Monet's paintings'
their arrival in Delhi proves that 'Naxalites are
a major' C the globe's anti-capital specific
to 'section 8' where a fusion of the aesthetics
becomes 'local news' however 'genuinely' people
are concerned about the rise of 'Islamo
-fascism' or 'conceptual erasure' of 'the intro
to nonmilitary kung fu' as long as 'indigenous
languages are dying' math will 'leave third
-degree burns' on the superficial flexible who
has 'gotten into calisthenics' southern athletes
performed far greater 'in this Olympics' though
sourced amino acids limit a weakened building
block 'poor synthesis' I'm curious about
the backdrop of 'ethnic meals' are 'imaginative'
'exotic' and 'transformative' the population
'prone to justice' but jaded & jubilant
so how hasn't 'the slow Wi-Fi' impacted
the marionette who contracts an oat a father sold
his heaven for the Quran cannot be passive
the wheat 'as a substitute for Macintosh'
programming to afford an equally beautiful
aquarium & nothing can be 'unrealistic'

the parenthetical is (internal)

      (perpendicular to)
underneath the burned bridge
a population at large   is addict
across the river   savor
the magnificent landscape of shit
the most widespread predictions
indicate scattered non-for-profits
      (future is alike)

by the laws of currency exchange
helmet wearing visitor brings a gift
      (later happens)
an inferiority complex   airy
as combed cotton   plastic
as operation freedom within us
      (walking in boots)
when we look up to India or Tajikistan

the seventh I left home   I played
Michael Nyman's   the promise
and one program director scanned
me for Afghanness then adjusted
his glasses a reflection in which
I prompted myself
      (do not take it
      as a compliment)

I've dwelled in a hypothetical
place of birth   I too wouldn't pick
these identification markers
so I count the tells when someone
says be yourself
      (of ten, nine times)
they're northern   not asked
what was wrong about my parents

the reasons we are stationed here
whose faults are collective failures
is the verb living differential
      (past in the most
      tragic way
      present)

travel for the national bourgeois is contouring within / an unveiling open-air museum the nerve forward: required

our perception assembles oral guidelines stuffing bullet points into the ears: moderate garments, leave national card remove the sim

an inherited technique: wrapping meat in naan confining it in a plastic bag flavoring a soggy bread making all parts of a meal   equally desirable

this is an experiment of forgiving: a pilot for free movement we had dreamt of backpacking in the valleys of Nuristan   in the woods of Kunar

every other year a visit to Salsal and Shamama was more dangerous   on this road   multiple exposed throats   urban and young

unproportionable beauty and wild insects   the deal was random but this travertine was as beautiful as any any I have seen not mine   except this

I know nature is not pledging a particular lineage   but   the   mountain connecting the land to this band   is an apparition distorted freezing and wary

Witnessed first in my casually Eid outfit en route to vacationing on the deep blue lake   the   canyon   of   our parents' snaffled   childhood

In the night before the television screened not its outline the piece of the puzzle itself by afternoon the rain never helped clarify   what   is   a ceasefire   my nephew asked fire is enough

two Talib walked toward our car then followed the pattern   putting   on lipstick my sister did not dare step out of the car   like a passenger in that minibus maintaining the straight stare the driver was not convinced to continue the   pause   how   this   exist my father exclaimed naked sins facing God   how could the medicine be effective after Sohrab is already dead this country is surprising

taxi drivers here talk of the rising price of   flour   understanding   peace   not procedurally as a dichotomy between absent and present things abstract in Kabul the prediction is a game one invests in and war wins frequently and when there are more agate rings on the opposite side of the table rumors claim Khalilzad   is   dead   the   American administration has changed

a baby goat is patronizing my night dream

the united nations of poetry rejects the full stop

a full stop   in the tongue's arsenal   a mallet chapandaz keeps   it intervenes
in every motion   enforcing a sentence   bonds paragraphs
through the separation of the varying verbs   then unifies them to co-exist
but in the eyes of the other marks   it's a ruthless authoritarian   imposing
a constitutional referendum

a portrait of dot   in its entrance   against guernica   &   the installation
of bani adam   every statement needs a full stop   a speech of my source of food
is pause   the freedom to talk   it tosses my stream of consciousness
onto the dark cavities of teeth   making me echo what comes through the ear
it gets routine order from the frontal cortex

conceals sentiments   that don't fit into a linear structure   with an amplitude
of my rejection fear   the fear of being called out   the violent
member of the group   when there's neither a time nor an interest I swallow
them   in a ratio of making shorter statements.   cubic & tend   not harsh
like ashes I passed through

or the goblins of human rights   as an object the terminal period is an ak47
pointed at my dictionary of pouring out   initializing the establishments
my therapist says   *this act is post-traumatic*   omitting stress drinking
from her cup   in my mind   I commute to a post office   where the letters
can be sent like a mailbox i'm emptied

disbound

I'm awakened to an atrocious dream: my sister cuts
her hand   an extreme amount of mist

        I can't make out
        the image

                        the scene has taken place
in the kitchen and as she walks into the living
the innocence of her one question hangs

            What do *you* think?

per the word of mouth
the solicitudes and the dis
-figured candidate proceeds

            At any rate, secure that delicate passage

Uneased, she asks if she could dhl this to my house
                        where I sit on my bed
examining my past and future

Two weeks following the dream

      a last province falls

           a coward
             president

  renounces the country

          midair

the dream

        follows the fall of a last
            province

         mid-week   flees
              a coward

         two fellows renounce their bodies

         mid   dream

          for a delicate passage

             precedes the scene

                 of fall

       extreme mist

          an imagine

             I examine

          amounts

             to

            nothing

This June in the Bronx with my partner and his oldest friend
we watched one episode of *exterminate all the brutes*

soon

The documents affixed themselves to the members of my family
haunting me in ways unbeknownst to my lover or the old friend

Why do my people submit to this treatment?

terror jackets

spit motherfucker

air-striked

curse

blood

sewage

I am

that lucky bird

Frying Pan Park

The foundation two years before the takeover registers
that four in ten would leave given the opportunity

    by opportunity

many, possibly, mean a dignified manner of conveyance
dignity, an intriguing practice

      to be off tarmac a given dignity a
      singular opportunity

for those whose command of a foreign language is found to be useful

          to write requisition after requisition
          claims such as "my so and so" "deserve" a) and b) also c)
          hereby I promise not causing you an injury

and for those whose eyes must behold heart-wrenching capture

          plane after plane taking off
          the burial ground of locals
          leaving behind most

      concurrent misfortune

To inhale parallel particles in the air

my firstborn brother
—whose healing depression surges
        across the heart's bottom—
abandons Bamiyan
adieu indigeneity!

our second sibling
—whose eyes have taken on
        the task of his tongue—
renders fear and welfare
welcome like a shrine!

our third a sportsman
—whose information includes
        not being on an evacuation list—
cornered in a crescent kick, he drives
from a few neighborhoods east

to arrive in an apartment where the sisters live
                where in a daydream I have painted myself
                with an elongated arm stretching across
                the continents to reach Venus's hand
                I create this tenderness to call them
                with spiritual prerequisites

                        I barely hear
                        any fully formed thought
                        a babble, vanquished
                        sometimes a child's cry
                        I try not to ask
                        what now and then

That intangible item, in and out of focus, hope like a sign of change
that everyone talks about, lives underground. It's not uncommon
for it to persist or have little resistance to a flow of despair.

I try to grasp—is it a possibility to bring them:

My patient question ciphers irregularly.

Like neutrality amassing only to blow up in anger.

Despite the predictable tendencies, I'm sorry.

For up until the last flight, I was worried about my persons.

The plural scattered and in silence chanted *god the greatest* in support of an army
whose bodies were left in four hundred beds   the nemesis press releases
                    cannot differentiate the dead's roots from its belongings

It's almost November

Two and half months of two-point-o

My husband whom I married in that invasive
August mentions in passing:

>   *I didn't expect us to suffer this much*
>   *this early into our marriage*

The world's wildest ideological practices

on that infamous
site
of

experimentation

I rehearse the sum of all interferences
and my own insignificance:

my forms oppose irresponsible innovations

as a colleague describes they self-emerge and self-suffice

Bare
and humbled by the bombardments
with no expectation of idiosyncratic
declarations

this poem:

fourteen hundred words plant the pledge
re-do, re-do

And even though I have stranded
many architectures of you

always there lingers an outline
of something I must get back to

When my father died

        the constables were *not* poets

a cruel variant was traveling through the houses

       —we had no procession of mourners
the killer banned all trends of grieving—

        Outside, maps of the opponents were advancing

his gravestone on the long list of

        soon-to-be-carved

if I ever go back

      I will find him

lying next to my mother

nameless, at last

I want to go back

my father has died

their poets have traveled

to the outer maps

their killers have banned

all trends of advancing

constables' cruel variant

fled from the country

a coward

carved a gravestone

for each house

to grieve a long list

of mourners

who had no procession

notes

The poems "notes from Kabul," "urban correspondents," "on-site com-
mands," "telephone calls from PD #3," and "incumbencies' dispatch" are
made of found language borrowed from Afghan social media commentar-
ies; Afghan local media videos of people in explosion sites; government
officials' speeches, tweets, and announcements; and eye-witness accounts
from radio and podcasts.

In "on our chest planes," the Farsi song referenced is "Leaving and
Passing By" by Bomrani. In "bombast: a Persian etymology," all the words
except the italics, prepositions, and to-be verbs have come to English from
Persian. In "funeral," the phrase "leafless garden" comes from a Persian
poem of the same title by Mehdi Akhavan-Sales. In "phantasmagoria,"
"three angels" is a reference to "Pariya," a poem by Ahmad Shamlu. *Patience
Stone*, referenced in "inverse of most stories," is a novel and film adaptation
of the same title written and directed by Atiq Rahimi.

The italics in "meta-variable" are borrowed from the Ahmad Shamlu
poem "Anthem for the One Who Left and the One Who Stayed Behind,"
translated by Jason Bahbak Mohaghegh; some concepts discussed in
"meta-variable" first appeared in Frantz Fanon's *The Wretched of the Earth*.
In "how everything should end," the italics are dialogue from the Iranian
film *Here Without Me*. The poem "the question" refers to an infamous
T adage—"you have the watch, and we have the time"—that was addressed
to the foreign forces.

Heartland theory, referenced in "proctoring," is a form of geopolitics
coined by Halford John Mackinder in the 1904 essay "The Geographi-
cal Pivot of History." In the same poem, "sandstone statue" refers to the
Buddhas of Bamiyan and "giant balloon" refers to the giant spy blimp
that oversees Kabul. In "the united nations of poetry rejects the full stop,"

Chapandaz is a buzkashi player and "Bani Adam" is a Saadi Shirazi poem inscribed on a handmade carpet displayed at United Nations headquarters. In "Disbound," *Exterminate All the Brutes* is a TV documentary series directed by Raoul Peck; the data that "four in ten would leave" appeared in The Asia Foundation's Survey of the Afghan People. "Why do my people submit to this treatment?" is a quote from a Zadie Smith interview for Louisiana Channel.

The poems "inventory," "the property of being separate," "the photography of home," "madar jan," "a diwan unprinted," "a distinctive duplication," "meta-variable," "stress & strain: a contrariety," "precedes essence," "the question," "proctoring," "the quotidian," "the parenthetical is (internal)," and "the united nations of poetry rejects the full stop" are part of a series focused on punctuation marks. These poems were written during the COVID-19 pandemic, which is why I perceived the punctuation marks as "essential workers" of our language systems. Their marginalization and universality are indicative of two things: our interconnectedness and the hegemony of European languages. But in either case, punctuation's fluidity in translation, assimilation, and adaptation fascinated me during the formation of this book.

Select poems from this collection have been included in the following publications: *Poetry* ("meta-variable"); The Asian American Writers' Workshop's *The Margins* ("proctoring"); *Pamenar Press Online Magazine* ("the property of being separate," "the parenthetical is [internal]," "inverse of most stories,"); *Atlanta Review* ("tea house"); *Pocket Samovar* ("the photography of home," "road trip"); *AZURE: A Journal of Literary Thought* ("a distinctive duplication," "the united nations of poetry rejects the full stop").

acknowledgments

Thank you, Nanay and Aqay, for the endless tenderness you showed me in a world where myriad people hurt you. For even though you were the recipients of various injustices, you didn't let me believe in total powerlessness.

Thank you, Halima and Zohra, for being the first free women I saw. Your depth and intricate personalities stirred my imagination and legitimized my poet heart. Thank you, Sarah and Kowsar. Because you looked up to me, I wrote tirelessly.

Thank you, Mowahed, Nosrat, Abbas, Mustafa, Mortaza, and Mehdi, for supporting my decisions and encouraging me to pursue literature.

Thank you, Michael, for learning my love language: Farsi. Without you, this life engine will cease working.

Thank you, Mark Levine, Elizabeth Willis, and Matthew Klane. To say I learned a lot from you is an understatement. Thank you, Emily Wilson, Fowzia Karimi, Prageeta Sharma, Daniel Borzutzky, Ghazal Mosadeq, and Maureen Gokey for supporting my work.

Thank you, Kabul, for your air and cafés: Art, Cactus, Simple, and Taj-Begum. Thank you, Zahra Mousawi, Reza Mohammadi, Shaharzad Akabr, Mostafa Hazara, Mujib Mashal, Hassan Fazili, Roya Sadat, Shahrbanoo Sadat, Asef Hossaini, Freshta Sadeqpoor, Farhad Majidi, Aylar Rezaee, Naweed Hamkar, Ali Abdi, and Khosraw Mani. You all inspired the production of this book without knowing.

Thank you, Scott Collins, Nancy Antle, Moriana Delgado, Anastasiya Uçar, and Azamat Askar for your beautiful friendship. Thank you, Romeo Oriogun, Tino Zhang, Kelsey Kerin, John Bosworth, and Cindy Juyoung Ok for your valuable feedback.

And thank you to everyone at the University of Iowa Press.

Kuhl House Poets

Christopher Bolin
Ascension Theory

Christopher Bolin
Form from Form

Shane Book
Congotronic

Oni Buchanan
Must a Violence

Oni Buchanan
Time Being

Michele Glazer
fretwork

Michele Glazer
On Tact, & the Made Up World

David Micah Greenberg
Planned Solstice

Jeff Griffin
Lost and

Hajar Hussaini
Disbound

John Isles
Ark

John Isles
Inverse Sky

Aaron McCollough
Rank

Randall Potts
Trickster

Bin Ramke
Airs, Waters, Places

Bin Ramke
Matter

Michelle Robinson
The Life of a Hunter

Vanessa Roveto
bodys

Vanessa Roveto
a women

Robyn Schiff
Revolver

Robyn Schiff
Worth

Sarah V. Schweig
Take Nothing with You

Rod Smith
Deed

Donna Stonecipher
Transaction Histories

Cole Swensen
The Book of a Hundred Hands

Cole Swensen
Such Rich Hour

Tony Tost
Complex Sleep

Pimone Triplett
Supply Chain

Nick Twemlow
Attributed to the Harrow Painter

Susan Wheeler
Meme

Emily Wilson
The Keep